The Spirit of
TRUTH
& LOVE

A Bible Study of First, Second, and Third John

"Grace, mercy and peace from God the Father and from Jesus Christ, the Father's Son, will be with us in truth and love."

2 John 1:3 New International Version

LaLoni Leffall
One Vessel of Hope

WESTBOW
PRESS®
A DIVISION OF THOMAS NELSON
& ZONDERVAN

This book is a work of non-fiction. Unless otherwise noted, the author and the publisher make no explicit guarantees as to the accuracy of the information contained in this book and in some cases, names of people and places have been altered to protect their privacy.

Scripture quotations marked (NIV) are taken from the Holy Bible, New International Version®, NIV®. Copyright © 1973, 1978, 1984, 2011 by Biblica, Inc.™ Used by permission of Zondervan. All rights reserved worldwide. www.zondervan.com The "NIV" and "New International Version" are trademarks registered in the United States Patent and Trademark Office by Biblica, Inc.

Scripture quotations taken from the New American Standard Bible® (NASB), Copyright © 1960, 1962, 1963, 1968, 1971, 1972, 1973, 1975, 1977, 1995 by The Lockman Foundation. Used by permission.

Scripture taken from the King James Version of the Bible.

Scripture quotations marked (TLB) are taken from The Living Bible copyright © 1971. Used by permission of Tyndale House Publishers, Inc., Carol Stream, Illinois 60188. All rights reserved.

WestBow Press books may be ordered through booksellers or by contacting:

WestBow Press
A Division of Thomas Nelson & Zondervan
1663 Liberty Drive
Bloomington, IN 47403
www.westbowpress.com
1 (866) 928-1240

Because of the dynamic nature of the Internet, any web addresses or links contained in this book may have changed since publication and may no longer be valid. The views expressed in this work are solely those of the author and do not necessarily reflect the views of the publisher, and the publisher hereby disclaims any responsibility for them.

Any people depicted in stock imagery provided by Getty Images are models, and such images are being used for illustrative purposes only. Certain stock imagery © Getty Images.

ISBN: 978-1-9736-3001-2 (sc)
ISBN: 978-1-9736-3002-9 (e)

Library of Congress Control Number: 2018906997

Print information available on the last page.

WestBow Press rev. date: 12/27/2018

Contents

Dedication

Burlon Jr., Burlon III, and Terrence,

No one knows my journey like you do. Thank you for being the force behind God to keep me pushing forward. Our trials have been many, but we have persevered because of the God we serve. I am forever grateful for your unconditional love for me. You have consistently encouraged me to be a better person and follower of Jesus Christ.

Chasity,

You are fearfully and wonderfully made by our Heavenly Father. You are our son's wife, our daughter, the mother of our grandchildren, and a valued member of this family. This Bible study is also dedicated to you!

Kennedy,

You are my first grandchild, and you have blessed my heart from day one. My prayer is that you will grow up to be an awesome woman of God who serves the Father well, and loves as Christ loves. This Bible study is dedicated to you especially!

Kylie,

You arrived just in time to be a part of this book dedication. What a blessing to hold you for the first time on the seventh day of your birth; God's perfect number. I am expecting and believing that you will receive every good and perfect gift from above. Yes, this Bible study is dedicated to you, too!

Acknowledgments

I would be remiss if I did not acknowledge Jesus Christ for all He has done to bring me to this place in Him. I am eternally grateful for His love, grace, and the many times He has forgiven me for my disobedience. The journey in writing this Bible study would not have been possible without the individuals He predestined to pour into me, such as my siblings, friends, and other family members who have inspired me along the way. However, I would like to acknowledge those individuals who impacted the writing of this Bible study specifically.

Thank you, Shirley and Steve Wynn for all the opportunities you made possible for me. Mama, I am thankful for the time you spent teaching me, *"Now lay me down to sleep, I pray to the Lord my soul to keep. If I should die before I wake, I pray to the Lord my soul to take."* I am very aware of the sacrifices you made for my siblings and me. I am certain I will never know the full extent of all you have done to make my life better. That is why I wanted your hands on the cover of this Bible study. Your hands represent for me your power, strength and protection that you covered me with. They represent the times I know you held me when I was sick, the times you cooked for me, fed me, and prayed for me. This Bible study is evidence of your fruit.

Rosie Lindsay, this Bible study began at your kitchen table, and now, it is done. Thank you for encouraging me to keep writing and making sure I stayed on point finishing what I started. Your prayers have kept me focused.

Sherrye "Lou" Willis and Rossye "ROC" Carroll, you have both held me accountable throughout this process. I appreciate both of you asking me consistently where I was in completing this Bible study. This was definitely a long journey for me, but you were both patient while encouraging me.

I would like to acknowledge Travis and Toi Angelle for their love and commitment for the book cover. I am humbled by your effort to make sure you captured my heart's intent of my mother's hands being depicted on the cover. Also, thank you Candace Fortson and Jean Wynn for your help with my author photo.

Barbara Triggs, Mary Jane Christopher, Donna McCord, Elizabeth Braswell, Jacqueline Gales, Patricia Walker, and Eleanor White thank you for your advice and constructive feedback. Burlon Leffall III and Donielle Griffith it meant the world to me that you actually did the Bible study! Hallelujah and praise God! Alecia Swoope, thank you for completing the first editing and proofreading of this manuscript. Resnee Johnson, thank you for your honesty and diligence to read this study and assess whether it was scripturally sound. All of you helped me feel confident in believing that I could publish a Bible study. You all are an author's blessing.

LaKischa, Toi, Travis, Nicholas, Candace, Camden, Payton, Braxton, Chandler, Kenya, Kingston, Alicia, Carmen, David, Miguel, Jenee, Ken, Jason, Joshua, Kenneth, Keon, Kyla, Jaiden, Kaelyn, Skyla, Kenneth, Kevin, LaKeeta, Ashley, Vanessa, Alesia, Dominique, Taiasha, Darious, Jalyn, J'siah, Michael, Michael Jr., Kevin, Rosslyn, Jamie, Joseph, Gerald, Derrick, Jerron, Jayla, and Christopher, not only am I acknowledging you, I am also dedicating this completed work to you. You were also the driving force behind me completing *The Spirit of Truth and Love.*

Foreword

I have known LaLoni Leffall for more than 45 years. Our friendship bond began in sixth grade band class where she played the clarinet and I played the flute. We've shared so many life moments together since 12 years old. I am eternally grateful to God for our friendship.

LaLoni has always loved reading God's Word. I remember her sharing with me how as a very young girl, she read the Bible to her grandfather. I also vividly remember the day LaLoni said the sinner's prayer and accepted Jesus Christ as her personal Savior in high school. When I look back over our lives, I can see God's hand leading her.

In 1996, I gifted LaLoni her first Bible study called *Experiencing God!* I remember our conversations during the Bible study about her experiencing God for the first time. We were so in awe to realize that God wanted to show us how much He loves us and loved us before the foundation of this world. *Experiencing God* Bible study transformed LaLoni's life forever. It was the beginning of her journey to experiencing God's love and truth through the Word of God.

LaLoni has done many Bible studies since her very first one. As a result of spending time in God's Word, God has matured her into an amazing Bible teacher, prayer warrior, and laymen counselor. She utilizes her spiritual gifts of mercy and teaching to help other women and children grow in their relationship with Jesus Christ. While working as an employee at a mission's organization in Atlanta, GA, she mentored and encouraged women transitioning out of homelessness to trust God in EVERY situation of their lives.

Today, 22 years after being introduced to the *Experiencing God* Bible study, LaLoni has written her very first Bible study – *The Spirit of Truth and Love*. It is a wonderful 12-lesson Bible study! The purpose of this Bible study is to help new believers develop a habit of spending time in the Scriptures and spending time in prayer and listening to God.

One of the things I love most about this Bible study is that LaLoni leads you through each day of study as though she's right there studying with you. I pray that this Bible study will encourage you as much as it did me.

No matter what the beginning of your life story or journey, God has a plan and purpose for your life. The only way we can know His purpose and plan for our lives is through a relationship with Jesus Christ. Many of us think attending church is the way we become a Christian. It's not. The way we become a Christ follower is by accepting Jesus Christ as our Lord and Savior and spending time in the Word of God. When we spend time in His Word, He changes us.

The Spirit of Truth and Love Bible study will bless you.

Sincerely,

Sherrye Willis
Founder and President
Alliance for Greater Works™

"Everything in the heavens and earth is yours, O Lord, and this is your Kingdom. We adore you as being in control of everything. Riches and honor come from you alone, and you are the Ruler of all mankind; your hand controls power and might and it is at your discretion that men are made great and given strength."

1 Chronicles 29:11-12
The Living Bible Version

Life is...

Definitely a journey. It is a journey that will present itself with numerous paths and forks in the road. The question is whether we will make it to our true destination without error? The answer is no, but with the Holy Spirit's guidance there is a positive outcome.

The positive outcome is eternal life (Heaven). Eternal life actually begins at the moment of our accepting Jesus Christ as our personal Savior. That is our moment of salvation, and it is marked in time forever. At that point, the Holy Spirit takes up residence in us, and becomes the guiding force in our lives.

Thankfully, through God's grace and mercy, we are forgiven for many sins and mishaps we make along the way. Unfortunately, we have not been given the timeframe in which we have to make this journey. Therefore, we must be on point and determined to live a life committed to Christ while we have time. We must live our lives with purpose and determination and with a set goal in mind. That set goal would be to live a life to honor our Heavenly Father.

In living a life to honor our Heavenly Father, we are destined to bear fruit along the way. Our bearing fruit is the result of us obeying His commands. In doing this, we will draw others to the Christ life as we have been drawn. We didn't choose Him; He has chosen us to bear "fruit that will last" (John 15:16, New International Version). We must set our minds to this plan.

How do we prepare for this journey? We must obediently and consistently study as we are directed in 2 Timothy 2:15 (New International Version); it states, "Do your best to present yourself to God as one approved, a workman who does not need to be ashamed and who correctly handles the word of truth."

We must study to show ourselves approved.

Dearest Friend,

If you are wondering what it means to be "approved," it means to simply have God's favorable opinion of your life. In that, you are not conducting yourself in a manner that you should be ashamed, and you are living your life according to the Word of God. In essence, you are living out and believing what you have read in the Scriptures.

I wrote this Bible study to help you learn some truth about who God is, who you are to Him, and to give guidance in dissecting Scripture. It is written as if I were engaging in personal Bible study on my own and sharing my notes and thoughts with you. With that said, I mostly study from the New International Version (NIV) because it is more reader friendly for me. However, I often reference different biblical versions, such as the King James Version (KJV). Please be aware that if you are using biblical text from the internet, it might be slightly different. (According to my pastor, Dr. Charles Stanley, New American Standard Bible (NASB), in his opinion, is the most accurate version of the original text.) I search for Scriptures that reinforce what I have read, and I keep a dictionary (preferably Webster's Dictionary) handy to look up even the simplest words. I meditate. I pray. I talk to God. I listen. I tell him if I understand, and I tell Him if I do not. Many times I have asked Him a question, and He does not answer immediately. No, I am not expecting for Him to answer me in an audible voice (although, it is possible), but through confirmation in my spirit. That confirmation may also come through Scripture or someone else. Nevertheless, I believe the times that he does not answer are the times He's telling me to wait and be patient. However, He always answers. Please be confident of that.

I believe that regardless of where you are in your walk with the Lord or your understanding of Christianity, you would benefit from this study of First, Second and Third John. I wrote it with the young adult in mind or for someone completing their first Bible study. I wrote it hoping that you would enjoy reading God's Word. My sincere prayer in writing this Bible study is that you would long for more time with Him during each day of study. I want you to thirst for God as the deer pants for streams of water (paraphrased from Psalm 42:1-2, NIV).

This Bible study consists of 12 lessons. Please take your time and meditate on the many Scriptures I have referenced and do not rush to complete a lesson. If you need more than one day to complete a lesson, please do so. My intent is not for you to just know stories, Scriptures or passages from the Bible. My desire is for you to know God, the Father, His son, Jesus Christ and the Holy Spirit intimately. You will have an opportunity to share a personal reflection and write a prayer at the end of each lesson. I would like to also encourage you to purchase your own journal and journal daily as you study. Each day notate what you believe God is saying to you, and how what you studied for the day has impacted you emotionally and spiritually. I have shared several personal journal entries of mine at the end of this study as an example. I have also included a page at the end of this study for you to journal your experience of working through The Spirit of Truth and Love.

You would possibly find this biblical study to be more enriching if you are studying with other people. If you are doing this Bible study as a family, I am praying that you enjoy your family time together. In doing so, you would have the opportunity to share your thoughts, revelations, insight and ideas with each other.

We are all searching for the truth, but we get there from different starting points in our life. I have found that all opinions can impact our desire to know God, trust God and believe He is who He says He is. My friend, start from where you are, right now.

Your friend,
LaLoni

Overview

The author of First, Second and Third John is the apostle John. He is said to be "the disciple whom Jesus loved" (John 13:23, 19:26, 20:2, 21:7 and 20, NIV). He also wrote the Gospel of John and Revelation. He was present during many of the miracles Jesus performed and he sat next to Jesus at the Passover Feast (Last Supper). John was present with Peter and James when Jesus went up onto the mountain top to pray and the transfiguration took place. (The transfiguration was when Moses and Elijah appeared and talked to Jesus. *Moses and Elijah were no longer living when the transfiguration took place* (Luke 9:28-36, NIV).

*The "James" that went to the mountain top with Peter and John is **not** James, the brother of Jesus, and author of the Book of James.*

Lesson 1

1 JOHN
LIGHT: PART 1

"If we claim to have fellowship with him yet walk in the darkness, we lie and do not live by the truth." 1 John 1:6, NIV

1 John 1:5-10 (NIV)

*"5 This is the message we have heard from him and declare to you: God is **light**; in him there is no darkness at all. 6 If we claim to have **fellowship** with him yet walk in **darkness**, we lie and do not live by the truth. 7 But if we **walk in the light**, as he is in the light, we have fellowship with one another, and the blood of Jesus, his Son **purifies us from all sin.** 8 If we claim to be without sin, we deceive ourselves and the truth is not in us. 9 If we confess our sins, he is **faithful** and **just** and will **forgive** us our sins and purify us from all unrighteousness. 10 If we claim we have not sinned, we make him out to be a liar and his word has no place in our lives."*

Notice the highlighted words above, do they mean anything to you? Do they stand out in your mind while you are reading? Go a step further and look up the definition of the highlighted word or words. Then share in your own words your understanding of what the word or phrase means in the above Scripture.

LIGHT

_____

_____

FELLOWSHIP

_____

_____

DARKNESS (DARK)

_____

_____

WALK IN THE LIGHT

_____

_____

PURIFIES US FROM ALL SIN

_____

_____

FAITHFUL (FAITH) and JUST

_____

_____

FORGIVE

_____

_____

One of the first steps in having an intimate, genuine relationship with Jesus is being honest about who we are. He knows that we were born with a sin nature, and that is why He died on the cross. His blood that was shed on the cross purifies us. He wants us to walk in the light with Him and fellowship with Him. We do this by asking for His forgiveness and accepting His righteousness. He is with us on this journey, and He is there to help.

READ: 1 John 2:1 (NIV)

Who speaks to the Father in our defense?

_____

_____

In the New American Standard Bible translation, the Scripture says "_My little children, I am writing these things to you so that you may not sin. And if anyone sins, we have an Advocate with the_

Father, Jesus Christ the righteous:" (Note the word "Advocate" is capitalized in this translation). What does advocate mean?

_____

_____

Do you see Jesus Christ as an advocate? Please share if you do or if you do not.

_____

_____

Jesus Christ is an advocate for each one of us. John 1:1-18 (NIV) expresses it completely that Jesus was with God from the beginning of creation. He then came to Earth to teach us, direct us, guide us and ultimately He died for our sins. After His resurrection, He ascended to Heaven and is presently positioned at the right hand of God (Mark 16:19, NIV).

Some Scriptures reference Him being *seated* at God's right hand and others *standing* at God's right hand. Nevertheless, He is there. He is rightfully in His place of authority with the Father. In John 14:6 (NIV), Jesus specifically says, "I am the way and the truth and the life. No one comes to the Father except through me." In John 16:23-24 (NIV), Jesus tells the disciples that the Father (God) will give them whatever they ask in His name.

Jesus is present with the Father interceding on our behalf.

In 1 John 2:2 (NIV), what does *"He is the atoning sacrifice for our sins"* mean to you?

_____

_____

In other versions, the Scripture says that He is the *"propitiation"* or *"sacrifice"* for our sins. Jesus took the punishment for our sins out of love for us. He took the blame for something He did not do by shedding His own blood on the cross. Jesus satisfied, through His death on the cross, God's wrath for our sins. He was the sacrificial lamb for us.

John 3:16 (KJV)

"16 For God so loved the world that he gave His only begotten Son, that whosoever believeth in him should not perish, but have everlasting life."

Jesus is the source of eternal salvation for all who obey Him (Hebrews 5:9, NIV). We know that we have come to know Him if we obey His commands. Obeying His commands can be challenging at times because we are imperfect people. However, Jesus is perfection, and if we have surrendered our lives to Him, we are more than likely to not feel alone on the journey.

If you claim to live in Christ, how would you or *should* you conduct yourself?

_____

_____

PERSONAL REFLECTION: Read 1 John 1:5-8 (NIV) several times, and meditate on it. What does 1 John 1:5-8 (NIV) speak to your heart? How are you feeling emotionally? Is it saying anything to you regarding your relationship with God? Do you want to change anything about yourself as a result of what you have studied? What does it prompt you to pray?

_____

_____

_____

_____

_____

_____

_____

PRAYER:

Father, thank you for

_____

_____

_____

_____

_____

_____

_____

_____

In Jesus Christ's name.
Amen.

Lesson 2

LIGHT: PART 2

"Whoever loves his brother lives in the light, and there is nothing in him to make him stumble." 1 John 2:10, NIV

"Jesus Christ is the same yesterday and today and forever" (Hebrews 13:8, NIV). He is the one true light sent to Earth in physical form to model truth in love. Scripture tells us in John 1:2 (NIV) that Jesus was with God in the beginning. He was there when our Heavenly Father created light on the first day of creation. At the point of salvation, after we accept Jesus Christ as our personal Savior, He comes to live within us. Therefore, His light has also taken up residence inside of us. The darkness of hate cannot live comfortably inside of us with His light. I read in an article that hatred is fear without courage. His perfect love drives out fear (1 John 4:18, NIV). Therefore, the love of Christ within us should eliminate any hatred we have towards a brother or sister.

READ 1 John 2:9-11 (NIV)

*"9 Anyone who claims to be in the light but **hates** his brother is still in the darkness.10 Whoever **loves** his brother lives in the light, and there is nothing in him to make him stumble. 11 But whoever hates his brother is in the darkness and walks around in the darkness; he **does not know** where he is going, because the darkness has **blinded** him."*

Write your understanding below of the bolded words above based on how they are used in the Scriptures.

HATES

_____

_____

LOVES

_____

_____

DOES NOT KNOW

_____

_____

BLINDED

_____

_____

If darkness is total absence of light, what is light?

In reality, light is total absence of darkness. The light can shine brightly or the light can be dim. The same concept can be evident in a person's life. The song that comes to mind is "*This little light of mine I'm going to let it shine.*" Is your light shining brightly or is it dim? Is your light on high beam or is it a soft beam barely helping others see the way?

The Scripture's reference to hate reflects a strong dislike for someone. Webster's dictionary defines hate as an "intense hostility and aversion usually deriving from fear, anger, or sense of injury." When *I* define hate, in the context of the above Scriptures, I think of an extreme dislike for someone. Hate is an emotion that results in someone not treating a person fairly, or saying or doing things that hurt themselves or others. Hate is a sin when directed towards a **person** negatively. It is not a true representation of Christ's love. However, in Proverbs 6:16-19 (NIV), Scripture states the following: "*16 There are six things the Lord hates, seven that are detestable to him: 17 haughty eyes, a lying tongue, hands that shed innocent blood, 18 a heart that devises wicked schemes, feet that are quick to rush into evil, 19 a false witness who pours out lies and a man who stirs up dissension among brothers.*" These are a list of behaviors the Lord hates, not people.

A person who does not know where he is going is basically lost. In the context of the Scripture, he lacks knowledge about what truth is, possibly because he is not in fellowship with the Father. (*John 14:6, NASB says, "I am the way, and the truth and the life; no one comes to the Father but through Me."*) The person's actions do not indicate that they are a follower of Christ, but are relying on themselves. In contrast, when a person is relying on Christ, they allow Christ to live His life through them. They give up their right to hate and allow Christ to control their emotions.

When the Scripture says that "darkness has blinded him," it is not a physical blindness. It is a spiritual blindness where one is unable to love as Jesus Christ loves. Christ's love for us is unconditional. He loves us regardless of the wrong we have done. He is always willing to do and give to us even when we do not deserve it. He gives us grace and mercy when it has not been earned. His love is sacrificial. John 15:13, New International Version states, "*Greater love has no one than this, that he lay down his life for his friends.*" Jesus is the Light, and because of Him we can see, feel and experience how to love one another as He loves us.

PERSONAL REFLECTION: Read 1 John 2:9-11 (NIV) several times, and meditate on it. What does 1 John 2:9-11(NIV) speak to your heart? How do you see yourself when you read the above Scriptures? How are you feeling emotionally? Is it saying anything to you regarding your relationship with God? Do you want to change anything about yourself as a result of what you have studied? What does it prompt you to pray?

_____

_____

_____

_____

_____

_____

_____

_____

_____

PRAYER:

Father, forgive me for not relying on you when

_____

_____

_____

_____

_____

_____

_____

_____

In Jesus Christ's name,
Amen.

Lesson 3

THE WORLD: PART 1

"The world and its desires pass away, but the man who does the will of God lives forever." 1 John 2:17, NIV

What a blessing it would be if the only challenge we experienced was trying to pass an exam to graduate from high school or secure employment. Yes, there are many challenges greater than these that can be traumatic. The longer we live and the more we experience life, there will be one challenge after the other. Even the hurt and pain associated with unexpected illness and death can be life altering. The unexpected can leave a person in a state of hopelessness. Feeling hopeless can result in deep sadness or depression. Feelings such as these leave a person feeling emotionally trapped, which is bondage. The symptoms of bondage are seen in a variety of ways: substance abuse, promiscuity, pride, manipulation and even habitual lying. Without spiritual and emotional healing, some people never recover from their traumatic experiences. God's Word is part of the healing process in breaking free from the bondage of life controlling issues that develop as a result of life challenges.

Our Father created a beautiful place for us to flourish. But, because of sin, we experience trials, tribulations, and challenges.

Read Ephesians 4:17-32 (NIV) and write your thoughts:

_____

_____

_____

_____

_____

_____

_____

Ephesians 4:17-32 (NIV) is an accurate picture of the darkness we are faced with everyday, but the Scriptures also clearly state how we can live in Christ every day. We experience darkness among our friends, at work, and even in our own families. That is not to say that any of these people are bad people, but the light of Christ may not be evident. We all fall short of measuring up to God's goodness (Romans 3:23, NIV). Like the Gentiles, we are living in darkness when we lack understanding and are separated from God because of the ignorance in us due to us having hard hearts. But, if we are truly in fellowship with Christ, we moment by moment, strive for living in the Light.

Once upon a time, what we watched on television (as a whole) gave us a hope for a better life. *Now*, entertainment, in a broad sense, taints the better life, and offers us the world and its views.

Ephesians 4:28, New International Version says, "He who has been stealing must steal no longer..." Of course, most of us would not consider ourselves to be thieves, but we have to be mindful of the small things we take that are not ours. Are we quick to claim an item we *find* as ours and call it a blessing, or do we try to find the rightful owner? How often do we give in to talking about someone in a derogatory manner, or sharing their downfall in conversation with others? Let us take a stand and build others up according to their needs, so that it may benefit anyone who is listening. I challenge you to keep a list of the number of things you see in one day that Ephesians 4:17-32 (NIV) identifies as darkness. Also, identify the times that you recognize light in the darkness. I am hoping that as you are notating darkness and light, you are always the common denominator in the light.

READ 1 John 2:15-17 (NIV)

What does "Do not love the world" mean to you?

_____

_____

_____

_____

_____

_____

Food for thought in response to "Do not love the world:" To love anything that does not have Christ's blessing stamped on it. To love anything that clearly is not in alignment with Christ and His Word. To delight oneself in anything that is not a true reflection of who Christ is. To love the world is to love anything that is clearly not the will of God for you.

1 John 2:17 (NIV) states, *"The world and its desires pass away, but the man who does the **WILL** (emphasis mine) of God lives forever."*

WILL: The power or capacity of free, conscious choice. The ability to determine or control one's actions, especially self-control.

1 Thessalonians 5:16-18 (NIV)
*"16 Be joyful always, 17 pray continually; 18 give thanks in all circumstances, for this is God's **WILL** (emphasis mine) for you in Christ Jesus."* (Meditate on this Scripture and memorize it.)

Fill in the blanks:

1 John 2:15-17 (NIV)

Do not love the world or _____ in the world. If anyone loves the world, the love of the _____ is not in him. For everything in the world—the _____ of sinful man, the _____ of his eyes and the _____ of what he has and does—comes not from the _____ but from the _____. The world and its desires pass away, but the man who does the _____ of_____ lives _____.

PERSONAL REFLECTION: Ask God to reveal to you specific things of the world that have held more of your focus than Him. What do you recognize gets most of your attention throughout the day? What worldly things have been more important to you than following the will of God?

_____

_____

_____

_____

_____

_____

_____

_____

_____

_____

_____

_____

_____

_____

PRAYER:

Father, help me to take my focus off of the things I participate in that are not your will, and help me to

_____

_____

_____

_____

_____

_____

_____

_____

_____

_____

In Jesus's Christ's name,
Amen.

Lesson 4

THE WORLD: PART 2

"But you have an anointing from the Holy One, and all of you know the truth."
1 John 2:20, NIV

Ephesians 4:17-32 and 1 John 2:15-17 (NIV) should leave us in deep reflection regarding the life we are living, and the things we are willing to compromise for our personal enjoyment. We must ask ourselves if our desires are more important than our love for Christ. Are we willing to take our light into the dark places just for enjoyment, or are we there to win souls? I would say that our heart's desire is to not enter into the dark places if we are not there to represent Christ.

Read 1 John 2:18-27 (NIV)

Is there one antichrist or many antichrists?

_____

_____

Who are the antichrists or what are the characteristics of the antichrist? (v.22-23)

_____

_____

Who is the liar? It is the man who denies that Jesus is who? _____. Such a man is the antichrist if he denies the Father and who? _____. No one who denies the Son has who? _____. Whoever acknowledges the Son has who? _____.

Read 2 Thessalonians 2:1-4 (NIV)

Jesus Christ's second coming will not take place until what takes place? (v.3 - 4)

_____

_____

_____

_____

Read 2 Thessalonians 2:8-11 (NIV)

Why do you believe the antichrist (*that wicked, man of lawlessness, evil man*) is not referred to as Satan, but one that will be in accordance with the work of Satan?

_____

_____

_____

_____

_____

The antichrist is any person who is spiritually dead and living his life in accordance with the work of Satan in Adam. Satan was present from the beginning in the Garden of Eden. He is an evil spirit and as real as the Holy Spirit. Satan works through man to wreak havoc on those willing to listen and obey. Satan wants us to remain separated from God, and sin holds us hostage in Adam. (Romans 5:12, NIV says, "*Therefore, just as sin entered the world through one man (Adam), and death through sin, and in this way death came to all men, because all sinned.*") This Scripture is not just speaking of physical death, but spiritual death that separates us from God.

Friend, when Satan was present in the Garden of Eden he tempted Eve to rebel against God. His temptation was to alter her thinking regarding God's instruction to Adam for them not to eat from the tree of knowledge of good and evil (Genesis 2:17, NIV). Adam was told "for when you eat of it you will surely die" (Genesis 2:17, NIV). Satan approached Eve in the form of a serpent, and she was enticed to go against what God had instructed (she rebelled). She then bit of the fruit and shared it with Adam. The Scripture says, "When the woman saw that the fruit of the tree was good for food and pleasing to the eye, and also desirable for gaining wisdom, she took some and ate it" (Genesis 3:6, NIV). Eve and Adam took their focus off of God, and placed their focus on themselves. This was defined as the fall of man, and because of their sin, we were all born into sin. Again, it is our sin that separates us from God.

I have a personal experience of Satan working through a man to wreak havoc on someone willing to listen and obey. That person willing to listen and obey Satan was me. When I was in college, a young man, pleasing to the eye, consistently wooed me. After months of flattery, he finally convinced me to allow him to pick me up to go to his apartment; well after midnight. When I arrived at his apartment he attempted to force himself on me. Only by the grace of God was I able to flee the situation. If I had been deeply rooted in God's Word and sensitive to the leading of the Holy Spirit, I would not have willingly agreed to go to his apartment. I would have boldly said, "Get behind me, Satan! You are a stumbling block to me; you do not have in mind the things of God, but the things of men" (Matthew 16:23, NIV).

Satan infiltrates our souls (mind, will and emotions) to move us to act on his behalf. Just as Eve was deceived by the serpent's (Satan's) cunningness, my mind was also led astray from sincere and pure devotion to Christ (2 Corinthians 11:3, NIV). The decision I made was not God's best for me. The decision to sin is always ours, no matter what Satan's influence is. Remember Satan is no match for God in power. God has all power (Ephesians 1:19-21 and Revelation 12:10-12, NIV).

Commit John 10:10 (NIV) to memory: "The thief comes only to steal and kill and destroy; I have come that they may have life, and have it to the full." Remember the thief is Satan or the antichrist. His goal is to secretively, without force, take control over your mind so that you will sin.

PERSONAL REFLECTION: What are you compromising in your relationship with God for your personal enjoyment? What area of your life are you allowing Satan to control your actions? Ask God to reveal to you any sin that may be taking precedence in your life. Do you want to change anything about yourself as a result of what you have studied in this lesson? What do you feel led to pray, or thank God for doing in your life?

_____

_____

_____

_____

_____

_____

_____

PRAYER:
Father, thank you for

_____

_____

_____

_____

_____

_____

In Jesus Christ's name,
Amen.

Lesson 5

THE WORLD: PART 3

"And now, dear children, continue in him, so that when he appears we may be confident and unashamed before him at his coming." 1 John 2:28, NIV

When we accept Christ as our personal Savior (salvation), we **enter** into eternal life with Jesus Christ. Jesus Christ was also there in the Garden of Eden from the beginning (John 1:1-2 and Revelation 1:8, NIV).

Read 1 John 2:28-29 (NIV)

What must we do to not be ashamed when Christ returns?

_____

_____

_____

How do we continue or abide in Him? Provide Scripture references.

_____

_____

_____

_____

It is easy to answer the above question by simply saying "I have to study my Bible and go to church." That is true, but there are Scriptures that provide guidelines for us to follow. Apostle Paul tells Timothy in 1Timothy 4:11-16 (NIV), to "set an example for other believers in speech, in life, in love, in faith, and in purity." Paul is establishing that as children of God we are people of influence, and we have the ability to impact lives. He further encourages Timothy to be devoted to reading the Scriptures. Psalm 119:11 (NIV) states, "I have hidden your word in my heart that I might not sin against you." This clearly indicates the benefit of memorizing Scripture. In order to know God, we must spend time learning what He says through the Scriptures.

Paul also tells Timothy not to neglect his gift. God has given each person a unique gift or gifts to be used in a manner that gives honor to Him. Paul further encouraged Timothy to be diligent in specific matters and to watch his life closely. In watching our lives closely, we must be mindful of the conversations we have and even the places we go. Paul made it clear to Timothy that what he did with his life would not only save himself, but others. The same is true of us. We represent the light of Christ wherever we go. Our actions and communication with others draw people to or away from Christ.

Colossians 3:1-17 (NIV) outlines guidelines for holy living, such as setting our hearts on things above. The passages encourage us to rid ourselves of anger, rage, filthy language, etc. It also declares that we are His chosen people, and we must show compassion, kindness, humility, gentleness and patience toward all people. As I mentioned in the beginning of our Bible study, *"present yourself to God as one approved, a workman who does not need to be ashamed and who correctly handles the word of truth"* (II Timothy 2:14-16, NIV). That is, study God's Word for revelation, growth and understanding. Seek out Scriptures to develop your faith and intimacy with Christ. (See suggested Scripture memorization list.)

Do I know with certainty that I am a child of God?

_____

If yes, what makes you confident of that belief?

_____

_____

_____

READ 1 John 3:9-10 (NIV) and fill in the blanks:

"9 No one who is born of God will continue to sin, because God's seed remains in him: he _____ go on sinning, because he has been born of God. 10 This is how we know who the children of God are and who the children of the devil are: Anyone who does not do what is _____ is _____ a child of _____; nor is anyone who does not _____ his brother."

We will never be perfect, but we can always strive for excellence in Christ by resting in Him. To rest in Jesus Christ means that we are allowing Him to live His life through us. With that said, what is your heartfelt response to the following Scripture? **"No one who lives in him keeps on sinning. No one who continues to sin has either seen him or known him"** (1 John 3:6, NIV).

_____

_____

PERSONAL REFLECTION: What area of my life am I in an ongoing cycle of sin?

_____

_____

_____

_____

_____

_____

_____

_____

_____

Take a moment to pray and ask God to free you from the bondage of sin(s).

PRAYER:

Father God, I come to you and I ask you to forgive me of my sin(s) of _____

_____

_____

_____

_____

_____

_____

Lord, I humble myself before you, and I cry out for your help. Lord, I ask you to remove any and everyone that stands in the way of me walking in total fellowship with you. I pray that you provide other sisters and brothers around me who would help me walk and abide in total love and fellowship with you. Lord, replace my sin(s) with purity and righteousness.

Father, free me from the bondage of sin.

In Jesus Christ's name.
Amen.

Lesson 6

LOVE: PART 1

"This is the message you heard from the beginning: We should love one another."
1 John 3:11, NIV

I accepted the Lord as my personal Savior when I was fourteen years old, but I never knew how or truly embraced God's love for me. I also began to question if specific people I loved truly loved me, and if my love for them was unconditional.

Scripture states that "we should love one another"…and that "anyone that does not love remains in death" (1 John 3:11, 14, NIV). Finally, I understood that when I accepted the Lord, Jesus Christ, as my personal Savior, I also accepted the Holy Spirit into my being. The Holy Spirit living within me means that I have God's love in me. I recognized through many heartaches that the more of Him that I allowed to permeate through me and in me, the more of His love came out of me.

This is "agape love." It is not based on your own strength and understanding. It is not based on circumstances or bad or good experiences with others. It is divine love for people.

READ 1 John 3:16 (NIV) and fill in the blanks:

This is how we know what love is: Jesus Christ laid down his life for _____. And we ought to lay down our lives for _____.

This Scripture is not referencing our dying on the cross as Christ did, but our unselfishly giving of ourselves to help one another. When I visited Ghana, West Africa in November 2006, the fullness of the above Scripture and the Scriptures that follow became reality for me:

"17 If anyone has material possessions and sees his brother in need but has no pity on him, how can the love of God be in him? 18 Dear children, let us not love with words or tongue but with actions and in truth." 1 John 3:17-18 (NIV)

I do not believe I have ever in my life felt such an urgent desire and longing to be of service to mankind as when I lived in a small village in Ghana for two weeks. My mission was to teach in the elementary school. The building was not like the school buildings in which I was accustomed to. There was no air conditioning, and it was extremely hot. The floors were cement and not carpeted which meant the heat radiated from the floor. The room had two windows, but there was no cool breeze blowing through. There were also no bathroom facilities. (The upper level students had classes outside directly in the heat.) Many of the children came to school with no shoes on their feet. I witnessed firsthand what it was like to live with an extreme lack of healthcare, clothing, and toiletries.

WRITE AND MEDITATE ON THE FOLLOWING SCRIPTURES:

Proverbs 14: 31 (NIV):

_____

_____

_____

Proverbs 19:17 (NIV):

_____

_____

_____

Hebrews 6:10 (NIV):

_____

_____

_____

Proverbs 22:2 (NIV):

_____

_____

_____

Proverbs 22:2 directs my thoughts to the analogy in James chapter two on favoritism. James makes it clear that in God's eyes we are all equal; rich or poor. He sums it up in verse eight by stating if you really keep the royal law found in Scripture, _"Love your neighbor as yourself, you are doing right." James 2:8, NIV Study Notes state, "the law of love is called "royal" because it is the supreme law that is the source of all other laws governing human relationships. It is the summation of all such laws (Mt 22:36-40; Ro 13:8-10)."_

Fill in the blank:

Do not seek revenge or bear a grudge against one of your people, but _____ _____. I am the Lord. Leviticus 19:18 (NIV)

Do not pervert justice; do not show _____ to the poor or _____to the great, but _____. Leviticus 19: 15 (NIV)

READ 1 John 3:18-24 (NIV)

"18 Dear children, let us not love with words or tongue but with actions and in truth. 19 This then is how we know that we belong to the truth, and how we set our hearts at rest in his presence. 20 whenever our hearts condemn us. For God is greater than our hearts, and he knows everything. 21 Dear friends, if our hearts do not condemn us, we have confidence before God 22 and received from him anything we ask, because we obey his commands and do what pleases him. 23 And this is his command: to believe in the name of his Son, Jesus Christ, and to love one another as he commanded us. 24 Those who obey his commands live in him, and he in them. And this is how we know that he lives in us: We know it by the Spirit he gave us."

Condemn – "1: *to declare to be reprehensible, wrong, or evil usu. after weighing evidence and without reservation. 2 a: to pronounce guilty: CONVICT b: SENTENCE, DOOM"*

How is it possible for our hearts to condemn us?

_____

_____

We are a triune being. We are a spirit; who has a soul (mind, will, emotions); that lives in a body. The soul is where we reason; choose to depend on Christ, and where all our emotions reside. Our spirit is who we truly are, and at the point of salvation, the Holy Spirit takes up residence in our spirit.

John is possibly speaking of our hearts condemning us when we allow our emotions or feelings to take precedence over the truth of what God's Word says. We cannot trust our feelings, but we can trust the Holy Spirit abiding in us to prompt us to respond to all things in love. Christ wants us to be confident about who He is regardless of what condemnation we may feel. Romans 8:1 New American Standard Bible says, *"Therefore there is now no condemnation for those who are in Christ Jesus."*

What does God command us to do? 1 John 3:23

_____

_____

How do we know that He lives in us? _____

_____

We will know that He lives in us when we exhibit the fruit of the Spirit. The first of the fruit being love, with joy, peace, patience, kindness, goodness, faithfulness, gentleness and self-control following (Galatians 5:22, NIV). Galatians 5:24, NIV, further states that those who belong to Christ have nailed their sinful passions and desires to the cross with Christ. In other words, they have surrendered their lives to Christ.

SUGGESTED SCRIPTURE FOR MEMORIZATION:

"I am crucified with Christ: nevertheless I live; yet not I, but Christ liveth in me: and the life which I now live in the flesh I live by the faith of the Son of God, who loved me, and gave himself for me" (Galatians 2:20, KJV).

Considering that I profess to be a Christian, the hardest question that I have asked myself is "do I really love Christ?" "I say that I am a follower of Jesus Christ, but do I love Him?" "How could I truly love someone that I never see, feel or touch?" "How could I love someone that I do not physically laugh with or take walks with?"

As I increased my time in meditation of God's Word, all the above questions were answered for me. Jesus Christ became real to me. I recognized that He spoke to me through Scripture, and I heard Him speak to me through the Holy Spirit. I have felt His arms around me when no one was present to comfort me. I have walked and talked to Him out loud because I know with certainty He is always with me. His love is in me, and I am in Him. I show my love for Him by obeying His commands.

God healed me when I was sick, He protected me when I was in danger, He calmed me when I was scared, and He used people to encourage me. On many occasions, I did not recognize Him. There is recognition of His presence that comes to mind now, and it still warms my heart to think of it.

I was standing back watching a magician entertain about 30 four to five year olds during a Sunday morning worship service. The magician made a dove appear out of a box that was assumed to be empty. The children were amazed and fascinated by the appearance of the dove. The magician told the children that she would allow each child to touch the back of the dove. Surprisingly, each child was fearful about touching the dove. Instinctively, one of the teachers walked up behind the first child and gently said, "I'm right behind you." Each child touched the dove because the teacher assured them that she was standing behind them. The room was quiet as we watched this teacher move from child to child assuring them that she was there with them. That was a vivid picture to me of Jesus Christ reminding me that through any and all of my fears, He says, "I'm right behind you." That day, I saw Jesus manifest Himself through that teacher by showing His love for each child.

PERSONAL REFLECTION: Can you recall a specific time Jesus Christ became real to you? Have you ever felt His presence at a time that you knew it had to be Him? Have you ever felt an inner peace or comfort that you could not explain?

_____

_____

_____

_____

_____

_____

_____

_____

_____

PRAYER:

Father, speak to me where I know without a doubt it is You. I want to see You in ways I never have before. I want to feel Your presence all around me. I want to be comforted in the middle of the night by Your love. _____

_____

_____

_____

_____

_____

_____

_____

Father, teach me how to love You.

In Jesus Christ's name.
Amen.

Lesson 7

SPIRIT

"Dear friends, do not believe every spirit, but test the spirits to see whether they are from God, because many false prophets have gone out into the world." 1 John 4:1, NIV

The Holy Spirit is the third person of the Trinity (God, the Father, Jesus Christ, His Son and the Holy Spirit). Jesus Christ told the disciples that He would ask God, the Father, to give us another Counselor that would be with us forever. That Counselor is the Holy Spirit. (Some translations refer to the Counselor as the Comforter or the Helper.) The Holy Spirit came into the world on the day of Pentecost (Acts 2), and the Holy Spirit was present with God from the beginning.

Read 1 John 4:1-3 (NIV)

How does one recognize the Spirit of God?

_____

_____

_____

How does one recognize the spirit of the antichrist?

_____

_____

_____

How is the antichrist a false prophet?

_____

_____

_____

The disciples asked Jesus what would be the sign of His coming and of the end of the age. Jesus told them to watch that no one deceives them. That many would come in His name claiming to be the Christ. (Matthew 24:3-4, NIV)

Write Matthew 24:24 (NIV)

_____

_____

_____

How do I know that the Holy Spirit lives in me? (Personal)

_____

_____

_____

READ John 14:15-26 (NIV)

Reflect on Jesus' promise of the Holy Spirit:

_____

_____

_____

_____

_____

The beginning of the Christian life is when we accept Jesus Christ as our personal Savior. We are born again by the Holy Spirit into the family of God. The Holy Spirit then indwells in us (i.e., lives in us). The Holy Spirit within us guides, directs and keeps us on the narrow path. When we love unconditionally, as God loves, it is from the overflow of the Holy Spirit. It is also from the overflow of the Holy Spirit that we bear much fruit.

How can I be sure I am not confused by the antichrist or those claiming to be Christ?

_____

_____

_____

I have read that the FBI trains agents to detect counterfeit bills by studying authentic ones. I think this concept would hold true for detecting the antichrist or antichrists (Satan). If we diligently study God's Word we will be more able to detect something or someone that is opposed to Christ. I know, personally, this is not always easy because Satan can present himself as an angel of light when in reality he is the prince of darkness (2 Corinthians 11:14, NIV). He is crafty and deceptive

(Genesis 3:1-13, NIV). He will oppose and will exalt himself over everything that is of God (2 Timothy 2:4, NIV). Satan will have the ability to deceive us with counterfeit miracles, signs and wonders (2 Thessalonians 2:9, NIV).

When I shared my thoughts regarding this with a friend, she said that Hebrews 4:12 "fell into her spirit". Hebrews 4:12 (NIV) says, "For the word of God is living and active. Sharper than any double-edged sword, it penetrates even to dividing soul and spirit, joints and marrow; it judges the thoughts and attitudes of the heart." This Scripture supports the importance of studying God's Word. The Word of God is one of the tools that will assist us in discerning (judging well) the true intentions of a person. His Word (Scripture) will equip us to have accurate knowledge about God when we are confronted with thoughts and attitudes that we question. Additionally, knowing God's Word will confirm if what we are experiencing, hearing or observing is the Spirit of God.

2 Timothy 2:14-15, NIV, implores us to present ourselves to God as approved. A workman who does not need to be ashamed and who correctly handles the Word of truth.

How do I know what is truth?

_____

_____

_____

_____

2 Timothy 2:14-15, NIV, places an emphasis on studying God's Word. The Scripture further encourages us to flee the evil desires of youth. Yes, when we are young we have more of a tendency to go along with the crowd. But, as we seek out the truth in God's Word, we mature as Christians regardless of our age. The Bible tells us the truth regarding the manner in which our speech, faith and purity should be lived out.

Matthew 7:13-14, NIV, says that the broad road with the wide gate leads to destruction. This is the gate that Satan has infiltrated. We discussed Satan's (the antichrist's) influence on the world during Lesson 3 of our study.

Be bold and strong enough to journey on the narrow path with the narrow gate. It leads to eternal life, i.e. the Kingdom of Heaven. You will find the truth on this path.

Write 2 Timothy 2:19 (NIV)

_____

_____

_____

_____

_____

Read 1 John 4:4-6 (NIV)

Fill in the blank:

4 You, dear children, are from _____ and have overcome them, because the ____ who is in you is greater than the one who is in the world. 5 They are from the world and therefore speak from the viewpoint of the world, and the world listens to them. 6 We are from _____, and whoever knows _____ listens to us; but whoever is not from God does not listen to us. This is how we recognize the Spirit of _____ and the spirit of falsehood.

What attitudes, behaviors, or character traits do the following Scriptures encourage?

2 Timothy 2:22-24 (NIV)

_____

_____

_____

_____

PERSONAL REFLECTION: How well are you being led by the Holy Spirit? Have there been times when you wanted to do something that you knew would not glorify God, and something nudged you to make a better choice? Did you later believe it was the Holy Spirit? Do you believe the Holy Spirit lives inside of you?

_____

_____

_____

_____

_____

_____

_____

_____

_____

_____

_____

_____

_____

_____

_____

PRAYER:

Father, thank you for the Holy Spirit. I surrender my life to You. I am asking You to bind any evil spirit that may be trying to tempt me to follow the broad path. Guide me in a way that I clearly know that it is You. I am praying for wisdom, knowledge and understanding that I will not be deceived by the antichrist. _____

_____

_____

_____

_____

_____

_____

_____

In Jesus Christs name.
Amen.

Lesson 8

LOVE: PART 2

"Dear friends, let us love one another, for love comes from God. Everyone who loves has been born of God and knows God." 1 John 4:7, NIV

I believe we disappoint God sometimes by our expression of love for one another, especially among believers. We so often live up to that which He hates most.

Read Proverbs 6:16-19 (NIV)

There are six things the Lord hates, seven that are detestable to Him. What are they?

_____

_____

_____

Read 1 John 4:7-12 (NIV)

If love comes from God, why do we struggle loving each other?

_____

_____

_____

When we see hatred, racism, murder, robbery, stealing, gossip, slander and the like spoken, exhibited or acted out, what does that tell us? See 1 John 4:8 (NIV)

_____

_____

_____

What do the following Scriptures say about God's love?

1 John 4:9-12 (NIV)

_____

_____

_____

Read John 3:17 (NIV)

_____

_____

_____

QUESTION FOR THOUGHT: Can you believe in God and not in Jesus Christ and be saved? (1 John 4:15, NIV)

_____

_____

_____

Why should we have confidence on the Day of Judgment? (1 John 4:16-17, NIV)

_____

_____

_____

In your own words summarize 1 John 4:19-21, NIV:

_____

_____

_____

_____

Around twelve-years-of-age, I knew that Scripture said that God loved me, and I chose to believe it. It was evident because of all He had done for me. He blessed me, protected me, and cared for me in so many ways. However, I could not determine if my life reflected my love for Him. My understanding of love was measured by my relationships with people that I knew. I believed someone loved me by the way they treated me - basically the way they made me feel. My love was then returned to them by acts of kindness and affection. So, I wondered if I really loved God because I could not see how I was showing Him love in return. 1 John 5:3, NIV, answered that for me: "This is love for God: to obey his commands. And his commands are not burdensome." We show our love for Him by obeying His commandments.

PERSONAL REFLECTION: If the strength of your love for God is measured by the degree to which you obey His commandments, then how much do you show your love for Him? Is there an area in your life where you feel sorrow regarding your behavior? What area of your life are you falling short loving others? Do you feel that you should repent, i.e., ask God to forgive you for your lack of love for Him or others?

_____

_____

_____

_____

_____

If you believe you should repent, consider praying the following prayer:

PRAYER:

Father, thank you for Jesus Christ. Thank you for what He was willing to do on the cross for me. I believe it was for me, and I am sorry for every time I have mocked His sacrifice by my willful disobedience. Lord, I repent, right now. My heart's desire is to be in total obedience to your commands. I do not want to be out of your will in defiance, rebellion or love. Father, I do repent for _____

_____

_____

_____

In Jesus Christ's name.
Amen.

Love,

Lesson 9

FAITH AND OBEDIENCE

"This is love for God: to obey his commands. And his commands are not burdensome, for everyone born of God overcomes the world. This is the victory that has overcome the world, even our faith." 1 John 5:3-4, NIV

People often question if they have faith because they have doubts. The biggest doubt, if people would openly verbalize it, is having faith in a God they cannot see. Hebrews 11:1, NIV, says, "Now faith is being sure of what we hope for and certain of what we do not see." I heard a pastor say that faith is not the absence of doubt; it is the means to overcome it. It is us moving forward in obedience to what we have read in Scripture or what we believe God is directing us to do even when we cannot see the outcome. Faith is trusting God when it does not make logical sense to you or others. Faith is standing firm in God's Word regardless.

What is your definition of faith?

_____

_____

_____

Read Hebrews 11:1-40 NIV

Write Hebrews 11:1 NIV

_____

_____

_____

Read 1 John 5:1-5 NIV

"1 Everyone who believes that Jesus is the Christ is born of God, and everyone who loves the father loves his child as well. 2 This is how we know that we love the children of God: by loving God and carrying out his commands. 3 This is love for God: to obey his commands. And his commands are not burdensome, 4 for everyone born of God overcomes the world. This is the victory that has overcome

the world, even our faith. 5 Who is it that overcomes the world? Only he who believes that Jesus is the Son of God."

Who overcomes the world?

_____

_____

_____

Scripture tells us that God's commands are not burdensome. What makes them less burdensome?

_____

_____

_____

What do you believe the connection is between faith and obedience?

_____

_____

_____

What is the victory that overcomes the world?

_____

_____

_____

Read 1 John 5:6-12 (NIV)

Who is the one that came by water and blood?

_____

What does the water and blood represent?

_____

_____

_____

When the Scripture references us being born of God it is talking about our acceptance of Jesus Christ as our Savior, and the Holy Spirit taking residence in our spirit. We are able to be obedient to God because the Holy Spirit dwelling within us gives us strength to do so. The Holy Spirit gives us strength to move forward regardless of our doubts. It is our faith that pushes us to be obedient and move victoriously, putting sin behind us. It is a day to day trust in God to do what is right by His standards.

Faith is believing (even if you have doubts) that Jesus Christ, God, the Father, and the Holy Spirit are one and the same. It is believing that water symbolizes Jesus' baptism, and blood symbolizes His death. It is believing that Jesus was also God at His baptism and at His death. It would not make sense to say that He was only a man when He died on the cross for our sins. Jesus Christ was the only one who could sacrifice himself on the cross for our sins because He is God made flesh.

Fill in the blanks: 1 John 5:6 (NIV)

6 This is the one who came by water and blood – Jesus Christ. He did not come by water only, but by water and blood. And it is the _____ who testifies, because the _____ is the truth.

Who are the three who testify? (1 John 5:7 NIV)

_____

_____

_____

What does that mean to you?

_____

_____

_____

In your words, what is the testimony God has given about His son (1 John 5:11-12, NIV)?

_____

_____

_____

Are **YOU** able to be obedient without faith? Why or why not?

_____

_____

_____

_____

1 John 5:14-15 (NIV)

"14 This is the confidence we have in approaching God: that if we ask anything according to his will, he hears us. 15 And if we know that he hears us —whatever we ask —we know that we have what we asked of him."

Under what basis should we have faith that God will give us what we have asked for?

_____

_____

_____

1 John 3:21, NIV, says, *"Dear friends, if our hearts do not condemn us, we have confidence before God and receive from him anything we ask, because we obey his commands and do what pleases him."* In other words, we cannot come before God expecting Him to automatically answer our requests if we are conducting our lives in a manner that is not pleasing to Him. Quite often He still extends grace and mercy when we are not living according to His plan. I call this His protection. Romans 8:28, KJV, states, "And we know that all *things* work together for good to them that love God, to them who are *the* called according to *his* purpose." We should have confidence in approaching God when we are in right standing with Him, and trust that He will answer if it is according to His will.

PERSONAL REFLECTION: What is standing in the way of your being obedient? If you are having a struggle being faithful, what is the source of that struggle? What is causing you to doubt? Specifically, what are you doubting?

_____

_____

_____

_____

_____

_____

_____

_____

_____

_____

_____

PRAYER:

Father, help me to believe even when I have doubts. Help me to believe when things do not make sense to me. I pray that the Holy Spirit in me will guide me to a place of obedience because of my love for You.

Thank you for the sacrifice that You made on the cross for my sins, and forgive me for my disobedience. _____

_____

_____

_____

_____

_____

_____

_____

_____

_____

_____

In Jesus Christ's name.
Amen.

Lesson 10

THE ONE WHO IS TRUE

"We know also that the Son of God has come and has given us understanding, so that we may know him who is true." 1 John 5:20, NIV

The ability to take a stand for what we know to be true is usually measured by our ability to support it with facts. We believe the sky is blue with splotches of white because we can physically see it. But, what about the blind man who cannot see? Does he believe it because many have stated it to be true? We believe that air flows in and out of our lungs keeping us alive. We cannot see the air. However, we believe with certainty that we are breathing it in and out. Our hearts beat at a steady pace (*and for some an irregular pace*) daily. We cannot physically see it, and under normal circumstances, we cannot feel it beating. But, we know that it is there beating inside of us. Our belief in something is supported by our own facts or testaments of others in agreement. God's Word supports that He is the true God and Eternal Life.

Read 1 John 5:18-20 (NIV)

What are the three statements in Scripture that reference what "we know?"

1

_____

_____

_____

2

_____

_____

_____

3

_____

_____

_____

Read John 15:1-17 (NIV)

Who is the true vine? (v1)

_____

_____

Who is the branch? (v5)

_____

Who is the gardener? (v1)

_____

Can you bear fruit alone?

_____

_____

Compare 1 John 5:14-15 (NIV) and John 15:7 (NIV):

_____

_____

_____

_____

John 15:8 (NIV)

"This is to my Father's glory, that you bear much fruit, showing yourselves to be my disciples."

How does faith and obedience tie into your role as a disciple?

_____

_____

There is no way I can call myself a disciple of Christ if I do not have faith in Him. I must (**we must**) be obedient to His Word. In Matthew 7:24-27 (NIV), Jesus tells the crowd that everyone who hears His Words and puts them into practice is like a wise man who built his house on the rock. In that, when the rain and wind came, the house did not fall. A foolish man does not put Jesus' Words into practice. A foolish man, in this sense, is not a true disciple.

A person who has faith in Jesus will acknowledge Jesus before men. Jesus will in turn acknowledge him before God, the Father, in Heaven. That is the character and action of a disciple (Matthew 10:32, NIV). Jesus acknowledged to the first disciples that the journey He was sending them on would position them as sheep among wolves. Jesus' Words remain true then and now. We must be able to take a stand just as Daniel did when he refused to abide by King Nebuchadnezzar's edict and serve his Babylonian gods and traditions (Daniel Chapters 1-3, NIV). In Jesus' own words he says, ***"It is written: 'Worship the Lord your God and serve him only.'"*** (Luke 4:8, NIV).

Scripture states, *"24 Then Jesus said to his disciples, "If anyone would come after me, he must deny himself and take up his cross and follow me. 25 For whoever wants to save his life will lose it, but whoever loses his life for me will find it. 26 What good will it be for a man if he gains the whole world, yet forfeits his soul? Or what can a man give in exchange for his soul? 27 For the Son of Man is going to come in his Father's glory with his angels, and then he will reward each person according to what he has done"* (Matthew 16:24-27, NIV). Simply put, it will be clear to God if we have lived our lives to bring honor to Him or to ourselves.

Matthew 7:16, NIV, states, *"By their fruit you will recognize them."* Our fruit will be the product or results of the things we have done. How many kind words have we spoken in Jesus' name? How many people have we led to Christ? How often have we served in the mission field? Although Jesus is speaking of prophets in this passage, I believe it holds true for all believers, specifically His true disciples. Every good tree bears good fruit, but a bad tree bears bad fruit. In the letter Paul wrote to the Colossians he encourages them to bear fruit in every good work, and to grow in the knowledge of God. Biblical knowledge is not just knowing facts, but having a heart for God that leads to Godly living. All of this comes by spending time with God in His Word and learning about who He is. A disciple is a *'forever'* learner; a student of Jesus the Christ.

PERSONAL REFLECTION: How are you living that brings honor to God or are you dishonoring Him in any manner? Do you desire to be a true disciple of Jesus Christ? Is your heart's desire to bear fruit? What fruit have you seen in your life? Have you led anyone to Christ?

_____

_____

_____

_____

_____

_____

_____

_____

_____

PRAYER:

Father, I want to be someone who knows Your voice. Please quicken me to hear You above all the things around me that are tempting me to distance myself from You. I come to You humbly, and I am surrendering myself to You to be Your disciple. _____

_____

_____

_____

_____

_____

_____

_____

_____

_____

In Jesus Christ's name.
Amen.

Lesson 11

2 JOHN
TRUTH AND LOVE

"Grace, mercy and peace from God the Father and from Jesus Christ, the Father's Son, will be with us in truth and love." 2 John 2:3, NIV

Read 2 John 1:1-2 (NIV)

"1 The elder, To the chosen lady and her children, whom I love in the truth—and not I only, but also all who know the truth—2 because of the truth, which lives in us and will be with us forever:"

Read John 1:14 (NIV)

"The Word became flesh and made his dwelling among us. We have seen his glory, the glory of the One and Only, who came from the Father, full of grace and truth."

Who is the truth?

_____

_____

_____

Write John 14:6-7 (NIV)

_____

_____

_____

_____

"6 Jesus answered, I am the _____ and the _____ and the _____. No one comes to the Father except through me. 7 If you really knew me, you would know my Father as well. From now on, you do know him and have seen him."

Jesus spoke the above words to His disciples when He was trying to comfort them regarding Him physically leaving them. He wanted them to know that He was the way to God, the Father. Not one of several ways, but THE WAY. He emphasized that if they knew Him, they also knew God, personally.

_____

Although Jesus Christ is physically gone from our presence, what does John 14:26, NIV, tell us?

_____

_____

_____

Read 2 John 1:3 (NIV)

Fill in the blanks: 2 John 1:3 (NIV)

Grace, mercy and peace from God the Father and from Jesus Christ, the Father's Son, _____

_____ _____ _____ _____ _____ _____ _____

Read 2 John 1:4-6 (NIV)

What has given John, the author of this book, great joy?

_____

_____

_____

What specific commands are given in these Scriptures?

_____

_____

_____

Reread 1 John 2:5-6 (NIV)

Read Matthew 22:34-40 (NIV)

What is your understanding of God's position on love?

_____

_____

_____

What is your understanding of the connection between love and truth?

_____

_____

_____

_____

The following Scriptures connect love and truth:

1 John 4:8, NIV, states, _"Whoever does not love does not know God, because God is love."_

Isaiah 7:14, NIV, states, _"Therefore the Lord himself will give you a sign: The virgin will be with child and will give birth to a son, and will call him Immanuel."_ Immanuel means God with us. If Jesus is God, then Jesus is love.

Jesus Christ states in John 10:30, NIV, _"I and the Father are one."_

Jesus tells Thomas in John 14:6, NIV, _"I am the way and the truth and the life. No one comes to the Father except through me."_ If Jesus is the way, the truth and the life, Jesus is the connection to God. God is truth. Jesus is truth.

2 John 1:9, NIV, states, _"Anyone who runs ahead and does not continue in the teaching of Christ does not have God; whoever continues in the teaching has both the Father and the Son."_

When we teach Christ, we also teach God, and the Holy Spirit is present in us as the Comforter who gives us guidance. It is imperative that we acknowledge in our teaching that God and Jesus are both love and truth.

PERSONAL REFLECTION: Where has God given me grace? Where has God shown me mercy? Am I experiencing His peace?

_____

_____

_____

_____

_____

WRITE YOUR OWN PERSONAL PRAYER REGARDING TODAY'S STUDY:

_____

_____

_____

_____

_____

_____

_____

_____

_____

_____

In Jesus Christ's Name,
Amen.

Lesson 12

3 JOHN
WALKING IN THE TRUTH

"Dear friend, do not imitate what is evil but what is good."

3 John 1:11, NIV

Read 3 John 1:2- 4 (NIV)

"2 Dear friend, I pray that you may enjoy good health and that all may go well with you, even as your soul is getting along well. 3 It gave me great joy to have some brothers come and tell about your faithfulness to the truth and how you continue to walk in the truth. 4 I have no greater joy than to hear that my children are walking in the truth."

Quite often we only hear of the integrity of someone's walk with Christ after they have passed away. Endearing words and sentiments are made after they have crossed over to the other side, so to speak. Is there joy in knowing that others recognize that you are walking in the truth? Do you feel a sense humility regarding that thought?

_____

_____

_____

_____

Are there others that you recognize who are walking in the truth? If your answer is yes, what evidence have you seen to support your belief?

_____

_____

_____

_____

Fill in the blanks: 3 John 1:5 (NIV) "Dear friend, you are _____ in what you are doing for the brothers, even though they are _____ to you."

3 John 1:5, NIV, resonates with me because it prompts me to examine my faithfulness to do God's work, especially on behalf of people I do not know. Matthew 25:35-40 (NIV) also stresses the importance of serving strangers while doing God's work: "35 *For I was hungry and you gave me something to eat, I was thirsty and you gave me something to drink, I was a stranger and you invited me in, 36 I needed clothes and you clothed me, I was sick and you looked after me, I was in prison and you came to visit me. 37 Then the righteous will answer him Lord, when did we see you hungry and feed you, or thirsty and give you something to drink? 38 When did we see you a stranger and invite you in, or needing clothes and clothe you? 39 When did we see you sick or in prison and go to visit you? 40 The King will reply, 'I tell you the truth, whatever you did for one of the least of these brothers of mine, you did for me.'"*

It is normal for missionaries to do God's work in foreign countries and within communities of people they do not know. God calls us all to serve people regardless of our relationship with them.

3 John 1:7 (NIV)
"It was for the sake of the Name that they went out, receiving no help from the pagans."

Who are the pagans (also referred to as Gentiles)?

_____

_____

_____

What message does 3 John 7-8 speak to you?

_____

_____

_____

Fill in the blank:

3 John 1:11(NIV)

Dear friend, do not imitate what is _____ but what is _____. Anyone who does what is _____is from God. Anyone who does what is _____ has not seen _____.

The pagans or Gentiles were those individuals who were not followers of Christ. However, the followers of Christ continued to show hospitality toward the men. They continued in this manner in order to work together for the truth.

In concluding this Bible study, *"Salvation is found in no one else, for there is no other name under heaven given to men by which we must be saved"* (Acts 4:12, NIV). *"All the prophets testify about him that everyone who believes in him receives forgiveness of sins through his name"* (Acts 10:43, NIV). God, our Savior, wants all men to be saved and to come to a knowledge of the truth. For there is one God and one mediator between God and men, and that is Jesus Christ (1 Timothy 2:3-5, NIV).

PERSONAL REFLECTION: How well are you serving others? How are you gifted to serve? How has your walk changed since you started this Bible study?

_____

_____

_____

_____

_____

_____

_____

PRAYER:

Father, I am thankful that Your Word gives knowledge, wisdom and understanding. I am asking You to give me an abundance of all three. My prayer is to serve You in a manner that makes it evident that I am striving to walk in the truth. My prayer is to serve You better by

_____

_____

_____

_____

_____

_____

In Jesus Christ's name.
Amen.

Dearest Friend,

I hope that you have found your path through 1ˢᵗ, 2ⁿᵈ, and 3ʳᵈ John to have been well worth your time. My prayer was that you would not have detoured or loss interest in this study. We are so important to God's purpose on this earth and the building of His Kingdom. I hope it is clear to you now that we are not just held accountable for our own righteousness and salvation, but our brothers and sisters, too. Although salvation comes from the Lord (Jonah 2:9, NIV) we must bear witness of its existence.

*God's will is that we are all saved and come to the knowledge of the truth (1 Timothy 2:4, NIV). We will not know the truth if we are not studying God's Word. So, we cannot neglect the call on our lives to do God's will in fervent Bible study. In being negligent, we fall short of His expectations. God is patient and **has been** patient with us. He does not want anyone to perish, but everyone to come to repentance (2 Peter 3:4, NIV). If we obediently make an effort, and ask God to empower us to do that for which He created us to do, we would live a life of holiness and excellence in Him.*

I was 14 years old when I accepted the Lord as my personal Savior. However, from that date to this date, I have broken all of the Ten Commandments (Deuteronomy 5:1-22, NIV). It does not matter if it were in action or thought, or to what degree they were broken. Sin is sin. What does matter is that I have found salvation and freedom in Christ. That is what I want for you, too.

There are several Scriptures from the Book of Romans that are often used to offer salvation to individuals. They are often referred to as The Romans Road to Salvation. As you read the following Scriptures, prayerfully consider making a decision today to accept Jesus Christ as your personal Savior, if you have not already.

Romans 3:23 (NIV)

"For all have sinned and fall short of the glory of God."

Romans 6:23 (NIV)

"For the wages of sin is death, but the gift of God is eternal life in Christ Jesus our Lord."

Romans 5:8 (NIV)

"But God demonstrates his own love for us in this: While we were still sinners, Christ died for us."

Romans 10:9-10 (NASB)

"But if you confess with your mouth Jesus as Lord, and believe in your heart that God raised him from the dead, you will be saved. For with the heart a person believes resulting in righteousness, and with the mouth he confesses resulting in salvation."

God's Word makes it clear that it is our sin that separates us from Him. His love does not change towards us regardless of whatever sin we may commit. He loved us so much that He allowed His one and only Son to die on the cross because of our sins. God will accept into His kingdom anyone that believes in His son, Jesus Christ. Romans 10:13 (NIV) tells us that everyone who calls on the name of the Lord will be saved. However, we must believe in Him in order to call on Him. And we can't call on Him, if we don't know Him. That is why faith plays a major part in our salvation. Romans 10:17 (NIV) tells us that faith comes from hearing the message, and the message is heard through God's Word.

My salvation came at the age of 14, but my freedom in Christ did not come until the age of 51. I surrender my life to Christ, daily. I make the choice everyday to stand on Galatians 2:20 (KJV): "I am crucified with Christ: nevertheless I live; yet not I, but Christ liveth in me: and the life which I now live in the flesh I live by the faith of the Son of God, who loved me, and gave himself for me."

Jeremiah 29:11, NIV, says, "For I know the plans I have for you, declares the Lord, plans to prosper you and not to harm you, plans to give you hope and a future." I assure you, God created each of us with a purpose in mind, and that purpose was to be His. He wants us to be totally committed to following Christ.

Read this Scripture again, out loud, until it becomes truth for you (and memorize it): Romans 10:9-10 (NASB) **"But if you confess with your mouth Jesus as Lord, and believe in your heart that God raised him from the dead, you will be saved. For with the heart a person believes resulting in righteousness, and with the mouth he confesses resulting in salvation."**

My friend, if at some point during this Bible study you accepted Christ as your personal Savior, please place the date here: _____

If you accepted Christ as your personal Savior prior to completing this Bible study, please place the date here: _____

Congratulations and Praise God!

One vessel totally filled with God has no alternative but to overflow with fruit and be free!

I love you,
LaLoni

LaLoni's Personal Journal Entries

My cousin, Charles, gave me my first diary as a birthday gift when I was a little girl. That small gift began the practice of my chronicling not only my daily activities, but my thoughts, dreams, and goals. Over time, it became what we now call journaling. Journaling helps me focus and sometimes it relieves any stress I may be feeling at the time.

I often express my feelings through rambling thoughts, prayers, and poetry. These entries are a gentle peek into my journey.

February 6, 1995

Choices

It was your choice to conceive me,
It was your choice to birth me.
Your choice to bathe and clothe me.
I know this was a costly fee.
There were many nights you sat up alone because I was ill,
Not once questioning God's will.
I must have been really sick,
For you to sit there and watch a clock tick.

Remember racing me to the door,
And I tripped and fell to the floor?
You picked me up and carried me,
Your choice to console me.

I remember being about this tall
There were children everywhere, wall to wall
All I wanted was a drink,
You didn't even stop to think
You lifted me where I could see
While I rested there on your knee,
'Kookaburra sits in the old gum tree,"
Your choice, you sang to me.

I had to be cheerleader, had to win
Just more money for you to spend,
And you were just my mother,
Not my friend

The hurt was bad,
And I could see in your eyes you were also sad.
However, your choice was to help me.
Help me get on with my life.
Prepare me for motherhood and being a good wife.

I took it all for granted,
Not knowing your seeds of love were being planted.

Now, it's my choice,
My choice to give it all back,
To give it all back to you because of all you went through,
I have no choice, no choice because I love you.

(I wrote this poem one day when I was thinking about my mother and my relationship with her.)

June 3, 1996

Sometimes

Sometimes love makes you want to scream out loud with joy
Sometimes love makes you cry and never drop a tear
Sometimes love makes you hurt so much you can't stand to live
Sometimes love can make you so angry you can't see the love
Sometimes love can be there and you can't see it or feel it
Sometimes love just stands there, and you can't put your arms around it
Sometimes love is so sweet and thick, you can cut it with a knife
Sometimes love is like water, it's liquid in your hands, and spills all over you
Sometimes love is so overwhelming, the excitement is ecstatic
Sometimes love fills your heart so, you can feel it throughout your body
Sometimes love is spiritual, and you can feel the ever presence of God
Sometimes love is so anointed you know that God is walking you through it
Sometimes love is just that… love…agape love

(This poem was written on a day that I was not feeling loved. My heart was aching.)

August 17, 1998

Lord,

I am completely, totally helpless and I thank you for your grace. I want to completely allow your Spirit to abide within me so that I will live righteous. I thirst for my rebirth in you. I know no one else can take credit for my salvation. Faith in Christ is the ONLY necessity to make me right with God. No human effort can contribute to my salvation; it is the gift of God. The gift is God's grace.

My heart is heavy today regarding my relationship with someone (name purposely omitted). I was feeling that my unhappiness with them was punishment for past sins. But, I know that God's grace does not punish you for sins. There is something else going on here…

October 6, 1998

(The following letter was written in my journal to my husband.)

To my husband:

I got up this morning around 4:50 am to pray for Terrence especially. The following Scripture is the first thing I read when I opened my devotional for today: "I prayed for this child, and the Lord has granted me what I asked of him. So now I give him to the Lord" (1 Samuel 1 27-28a, New International Version).

Now, I thought, "How appropriate; just like God!"

I began to pray and I started crying and telling God that I didn't know what to do for Terrence. He is eight years old and struggling academically in school! I am doing everything that I think I am supposed to do. I began praying and asking God to help me with him. I prayed that over and over. I even asked Him to show me what we needed to do. Then I acknowledged that I have prayed the same prayers repeatedly, and I still don't feel that we are helping him. I guess you ask where my faith is. Well, in my mind I don't think my faith is in question. I think my conversations with God give me strength to keep trying each day.

Finally, I just told God that I didn't know how to pray about this, and I started crying even more. Then it was as if God said to me "Give him back to Me." At that moment, I remembered the Scripture I had just read. I cannot explain it, but I began telling God that I would give Terrence back to Him; that I would give both my children to Him. What surprised me was that I was crying as if I was giving my children up for adoption. Then I started praying for all children who are struggling in some way or another. Again, it was as if the Holy Spirit said to me *"Parent's don't know how to give them back to Him."*

The word "dedicate" kept dropping in my mind. I told God that I didn't know how to dedicate my children to Him. I know that I am teaching them about God, trying to raise them to be Christians, and praying daily that they both be Godly men. God then reminded me of the story behind the Scripture above…Hannah had prayed for a child, and because God gave her Samuel she gave him back to God for His service. She literally left her child with someone else to train him to serve God.

I then remembered that it was Terrence who we tried over and over to conceive. I am not comparing him to Samuel, but I just realized that God actually gave me the "desires of my heart." It never crossed my mind to give him back to God. I asked God how I "dedicate" my children to Him. I asked Him if it was the ceremony they do in church? The answer is no; that is not it. Also, I do not intend to leave them anywhere for someone else to train. I believe the answer to me was that I dedicate them to Him by teaching them how to be of service to Him.

I believe that that revelation, if you want to call it that, was for a bigger purpose. We, as mothers and fathers, always pray and ask God to help us in rearing our children. But, they are not ours at all, they are His. I think if we can spiritually give them back to Him, and teach them how to be of service to Him, we have reached a holy and wholesome understanding of parenting. I can't explain it, but it is more than having them serve on the youth usher board.

November 25, 1998

When God Opened His Door

When God opened His door
The sun burst through the clouds
And rivers of water flowed from me
Like honey from its comb
The warmth in my heart
Soothed me like the softness of the clouds
His holiness lifted me
In the gentleness of His arms
And I rested

(Written on the road to Texas from Tennessee; inspired by the beautiful sky, and when Terrence said, "Mommy, it looks like God opened His door.")

February 16, 2000

Thank you, God, for the freedom and choice to serve you out of love. I am not serving you out of fear or merit-seeking. It is my heart that wants to serve you because you give me that choice. My desire is that I am a vessel you can work through.

November 25, 2004

Today, I got a new Bible! I truly wanted it <u>today</u>. I don't know, I think today is my turning point day. This is my "new beginning" day. With everything going on in my life – I recognize and I acknowledge that I am so thankful. I have so much! I have things and stuff people spend a lifetime praying for. At the top of that list is my family. I cannot even begin to list all I am thankful for regarding them…the laughter we share; the things we have in common…Father, I guess I just want to say thank you for making me a wife and mother. Those are two roles that I know were gifts from you. I am so thankful! Daily, I strive to be a Proverbs 31 woman. I want to be a woman who my children will one day rise up and call me blessed. I want to be a woman who will be praised by her husband. I want to be a woman who you are pleased with, my Lord.

Father, thank you for loving me.

September 3, 2008

My thoughts this morning were regarding the three men Jesus took on the Mount of Transfiguration with Him before He was crucified. This was very personal for Him. You see, He had twelve disciples, but He only chose Peter, James and John to share this experience with Him. My thought was who would my three people be? Who would your three people be?

I also thought of my sons and how I have their back in all things. But, I also have their front, especially if they are right. That means that I will go into battle ahead of them.

Who has your back and more importantly, who has your front? In all things; however, trust that God has you covered all around. He will go ahead of you and stand behind you at the same time!

September 4, 2008

"Whatever you do, do your work heartedly, as for the Lord, rather than for man, knowing that it is the Lord Jesus Christ, whom you serve. For it is from Him that we receive the reward of the inheritance"
(Colossians 3:23-24, New International Version)

Sometimes, I struggle with "working" when I'm tired or just feel unappreciated. It is during those times that I reflect on that Scripture. I am reminded that what I do has everything to do with what God expects of me.

We often expect and want accolades from man for practically everything we do. But, if we live out that Scripture at all times, we would operate at a level of excellence at all times without expectations of recognition.

In essence, everything we do paid or unpaid would be done with discipline, honor, and integrity.

I guess my point is that if we do all things as unto God, we would always be proud of our accomplishments regardless of any recognition from anyone.

September 5, 2008

I was lying in bed this morning really dreading getting up. So, I asked myself, "Why am I getting up?" "What purpose would my life serve in my getting up?" Then I concluded that I just wanted to sleep a little longer.

That is what most people do awake—walk around asleep. So, I really pondered what my getting up, waking up, should mean. What comes to mind is the Scripture in Jeremiah that says, "He knew me before I was formed in my mother's womb."

Yes, He created you and me with something specific in mind. We have a definite purpose for being here, and we should live each day like that, on purpose. Every decision we make should be moving us closer to our specific purpose, whatever that is—and if you don't know...maybe that is your assignment every day...

LIVING LIFE AWAKE...Seeking purpose in your being AWAKE...Keeping in mind that tomorrow could very well be your last day to do so.

July 29, 2009

Father,

Things seem so bad. So many relationships have changed in my life. It saddens me. Please step in and heal my heart. Heal their hearts. Help us to love and commune with each other the way you would have us to. Help me, Lord, to discipline my tongue and my behavior. I am asking you this in the name of the Lord Jesus Christ of Nazareth.

August 19, 2009

Lord, please forgive me for my loose tongue. Please help me to stop talking about my frustrations to people. Help me, God, to respond wisely and in a Christ-like manner when anyone comes to me with negative, ungodly conversations. Help me, Lord, to redeem myself in your eyes and my co-workers. I admit I have been wrong and disloyal.

Please forgive me.

November 15, 2010

This morning I got up and studied Psalm 103. This Psalm encourages me to praise the Lord. Right now, that is what I need to do. I have been playing praise music all morning, and I am not watching television. I talked to my girlfriend this morning, too. Her call was a blessing. She said that a relative died, and he died while singing.

Today is a hard day for me. It is another one of those days that I am struggling with my relationship with family members. It is truly hard for me to accept the disconnect they feel with me. I can only assume it has to be me. I brought this on myself somehow. It will also have to be me to just let go and move on. I have to. This hurt is so heavy on me. I must be compassionate, merciful, slow to anger and abounding in love through this.

The Lord works righteousness and justice for all the oppressed. That is what it said in Psalm 103:6.

December 13, 2010

LaLoni,

1. Stop confusing pride with confidence.
2. Stop giving people power over you only God should have.
3. Give God time to turn some trash to treasure. He will give you beauty for ashes! Trust Him, LaLoni!
4. Remember the victories that you and God have had together. God has seen every effort you have made.
5. When God sends encouragement, LaLoni, receive it! You must receive it!
6. Remember, God really loves you.
7. Love yourself.

April 24, 2011

Easter Sunday was awesome! Pastor Stanley preached the sermon I thought should be given if you had a packed house. This is so ironic! I had just told Burlon (my husband) before we left for church that preachers use Easter Sunday and Mother's Day to speak sarcastically about people not showing up for church service until those days. Pastor Stanley took advantage of the opportunity in a positive way to minister to all the people present that morning. He talked about NOT how *long* we live, but *how* we are living. He spoke of our citizenship in Heaven. He asked if our names would be recorded in Heaven in the Lamb's Book of Life. He talked about where our loved ones are that died in Christ. He talked about being absent from the body and present with the Lord. He said that our inheritance is in Heaven, our reward is in Heaven, and our treasures are in Heaven. Pastor Stanley said that everyone that believes in Christ will have eternal life, and God will raise us up on the last day. We don't know the date of Christ's return, but until then, we must be steadfast, unmovable, and know that our toil is not in vain.

Pastor Stanley became emotional when he talked about his mom, but he always smiles when he tells us she would always say to him, "Don't you be doing anything you don't want to be doing when Jesus comes." I will try to live by that, too. I also went to Passover Seder. That was the first time I had experienced it with people who were Jewish followers of Christ.

I am getting at peace with too many things…I hope that is good.

May 29, 2011

I choose not to let Satan get the victory in this. He has always gone after me to defeat me through my family. Thank you, God, for wise people in my life who will tell me the truth about me. I almost let go of what I know is "of God" because I wanted to take my final stand and walk away. Scripture says, "Satan's position is to steal, kill and destroy, i.e., families and anything that can be destroyed. I was getting ready to destroy everything that is sacred to me. What I had in mind would have destroyed emotionally everyone around me or at least caused some discord for a period of time. How could I be the woman of God I profess to be and do that?

Yes, I will be still and let You take control. But, show me what "being still" means. Show me how to love when I don't feel loved.

I love you for loving me, and I am glad I am here, really.

February 12, 2012

Father,

I was thinking…Who are people without Christ? I personally know people who have not accepted Christ as their personal Savior. Do they ever think about it? I know I am constantly looking at myself in the mirror questioning whether I am living obediently to God's Word. It makes me sad that some people may not even glimpse in the mirror. My heart aches. Whitney Houston died last night. I am praying that her death will draw many to Christ. I pray that Whitney was well with God when she left here.

March 17, 2012

I read about Deborah in the book of Judges today. Wow! She was the only woman to be a judge over Israel. Chapter five is a song written by Deborah or someone else. The song highlights battle victories. I was thinking…I want to live my life in such a manner that someone would want to sing an awesome song about it. A great song that highlights all the battles I have won. Maybe my song would encourage someone to stay on the battle field.

July 26, 2012

I just had a conversation with a friend about my obedience and discipline. I told them that God had changed my perspective on it. I was getting a little sick of people complimenting me on my obedience and my discipline. Some tell me that they wish they were obedient and disciplined like me. I fail a lot! Plus, it is <u>not</u> me anymore! I am yielding those character traits to God. I am seeking the Holy Spirit to do this "thing" through me. I am actively recognizing a Holy God behind all that I am capable of doing. I want to be led to complete and succeed at things because of the Christ in me, not solely because of my natural tendencies.

September 26, 2012

This morning I read Oswald Chamber's devotion titled "The Go of Reconciliation." This passage brought up a period of my life in 1997, when I was fed up with all the things different ones had done to hurt me. (I was also doing my first in-depth Bible study during that time. It was <u>Experiencing God</u> by Henry T. Blackaby and Claude King.) Just like God, He flipped the script on me! He brought to my attention all the people that I had hurt. He literally took me all the way back to elementary school. I was definitely hearing Him speak to me and direct my steps in a way I had not prior. I know that my recollection of thoughts had to do with the <u>Experiencing God</u> Bible study.

Needless to say, the way He instructed me, I did not expect. I forgave the people who hurt me, and I tracked down as many of the people as I could that I thought I had hurt. (I am positive I have missed quite a few.) God did instruct me "down to the smallest detail" as Chambers said. I found myself apologizing to 'adults' for things I did to them when we were children. I initially thought my apologies would appear childish and silly, but the response from people was very touching.

My actions (apologies) had nothing to do with me trying to be a saint or clear my conscious before going to the altar or worse: dying. But, there was definitely reconciliation and respect built between me and those I offended.

They say that when you know better, you do better. I would like to say that I know better now, and I am more careful about how I treat people.

November 27, 2012

There is nothing more tragic than to come to the end of life and know we have been on the wrong course. We have only one life to live down here, and we are free to do as we please with it, but if we seek our own pleasure, our life will never glorify God. We can live a life of holiness, for it is not our own life that has been changed, but the life of God that has been imparted to us. The Holy Spirit has been poured out on us. But it is not poured out on us to prove how great we are, but to prove the greatness of Jesus Christ.

September 16, 2014

1. Do I know what I am called to do?
2. Am I being taught by God?
3. Am I teaching someone else about Him?
4. Am I leading by example?
5. Do I feel that God is impossible to please?
6. Is it impossible to displease Him?
7. LaLoni, are you truly a dwelling place for His Spirit?

Father, sometimes I catch myself reacting to things and not coming to you first. This seems to happen a lot at work. Please help me to be quiet and listen for your direction. Am I where you want me to be in my vocation?

July 17, 2017

Am I a true Christian? Am I a born again Christian? Am I a cosmetic Christian? Am I who I say I am? Do I walk in truth? Am I a fraud? Am I a fake? Do I look like who I say I am inside? Do I present one way, but inside I am totally different?

Father, I want you to abide in me – in my spirit and in my soul. I want my body to act and move based on who I am inside. Holy Spirit please rest inside of me totally and completely!

March 25, 2018

My son suggested to me last night that I should read the book of Esther. He said this based on a conversation we were having. I verbally acknowledged what he said, but in my head I said, "I already know what Esther is about." This morning when I went into my prayer closet (literally) my devotion was on Esther. Shortly after that, I received an e-mail from a friend and her short words of encouragement were from the book of Esther. Later that morning, I received a text message from a friend about the book of Esther. Wow! It sounds like the Father wants me to read Esther. So, that is what I am going to do.

After reading Esther it became clear to me why Father kept putting Esther before me. He wants me to trust Him for the victory. He doesn't want me to fret when someone is scheming and attempting to manipulate behind the scenes like Haman was doing. He tried to kill Mordecai and the Jewish people, but he ended up being killed in the end. I have to keep my thoughts focused on God and not be so focused on how aware I am of what someone may be doing to bring harm to me.

I will trust God for protection for my family and me.

March 26, 2018

It is God who purposes everything in our lives. Even when we set our alarm clocks to wake us… something magical happens in the Heavenlies. The alarm clock goes off, but it is God who says, "Wake up, LaLoni." It is in knowing Him that gives me the grace to endure all things. He is my "Yes" when I am thinking it won't happen. He is my "Yes" when I wonder if anyone truly loves me with an unconditional love. He says, "Yes, I do. I love you, LaLoni."

I pray excerpts from my personal journals have blessed and encouraged you.

One Vessel of Hope,
LaLoni

My Personal Journal Entry of my Experience of The Spirit of Truth and Love

How has this study changed my walk with Christ?

_____

_____

_____

_____

_____

_____

_____

_____

_____

_____

_____

_____

_____

_____

_____

_____

_____

_____

_____

_____

_____

_____

Scripture Memorization List

Leviticus 19:15 (New International Version) Do not pervert justice; do not show partiality to the poor or favoritism to the great, but judge your neighbor fairly.

Leviticus 19:18 (New International Version) Do not seek revenge or bear a grudge against one of your people, but love your neighbor as yourself. I am the Lord.

Psalm 119:11 (New International Version) Your word have I treasured in my heart, that I may not sin against you.

Proverbs 6:16-19 (New International Version) There are six things the Lord hates, seven that are detestable to him: haughty eyes, a lying tongue, hands that shed innocent blood, a heart that devises wicked schemes, feet that are quick to rush into evil, a false witness who pours out lies and a man who stirs up dissension among brothers.

Proverbs 14:31 (New International Version) He who oppresses the poor shows contempt for their Maker, but whoever is kind to the needy honors God.

Proverbs 19:17 (New International Version) He who is kind to the poor lends to the Lord, and he will reward him for what he does.

Proverbs 22:2 (New International Version) Rich and poor have this in common: The Lord is the Maker of them all.

Matthew 16:23 (New International Version) Jesus turned and said to Peter, "Get behind me Satan! You are a stumbling block to me; you do not have in mind the things of God, but the things of men."

Matthew 24:24 (New International Version) For false Christs and false prophets will appear and perform great signs and miracles to deceive even the elect—if that were possible.

John 3:17 (New International Version) For God did not send his Son into the world to condemn the world, but to save the world through him.

John 10:10 (New International Version) The thief comes only to steal and kill and destroy; I have come that they may have life, and have it to the full.

John 14:6 (New International Version) Jesus answered: "I am the way and the truth and the life, No one comes to the Father except through me…"

Romans 8:1 (New International Version) Therefore, there is now no condemnation for those who are in Christ Jesus.

Romans 10:9-10 (New American Standard Bible Version) But if you confess with your mouth Jesus as Lord, and believe in your heart that God raised him from the dead, you will be saved. For with the heart a person believes resulting in righteousness, and with the mouth he confesses resulting in salvation.

Romans 13:8-10 (New International Version) Let no debt remain outstanding, except the continuing debt to love one another, for he who loves his fellowman has fulfilled the law. The commandments, "Do not commit adultery," "Do not murder," "Do not steal," "Do not covet," and whatever other commandment there may be, are summed up in this one rule: "Love your neighbor as yourself." Love does no harm to its neighbor. Therefore love is the fulfillment of the law.

2 Corinthians 11:14-15 (New International Version) And no wonder, for Satan himself masquerades as an angel of light. It is not surprising, then, if his servants masquerade as servants of righteousness. Their end will be what their actions deserve.

Galatians 2:20 (King James Version) I am crucified with Christ; nevertheless I live; yet not I, but Christ liveth in me: and *the life* which I now live in the flesh I live by the faith of the Son of God, who loved me and gave himself for me.

Galatians 5:22-23 (New International Version) But the fruit of the spirit is love, joy, peace, patience, kindness, goodness, faithfulness, gentleness and self-control. Against such things is no law.

Ephesians 4:29 (New International Version) Do not let any unwholesome talk come out of your mouths, but only what is helpful for building others up according to their needs, that it may benefit those who listen.

1 Thessalonians 5:16-18 (New International Version) Be joyful always; pray continually; give thanks in all circumstances, for this is God's will for you in Christ Jesus.

1 Timothy 4:11-16 (New International Version) Command and teach these things. Don't let anyone look down on you because you are young, but set an example for the believers in speech, in life, in love, in faith and in purity. Until I come, devote yourself to the public reading of Scripture, to preaching and to teaching. Do not neglect your gift, which was given you through a prophetic message when the body of elders laid their hands on you. Be diligent in these matters; give yourself wholly to them, so that everyone may see your progress. Watch your life and doctrine closely. Persevere in them, because if you do, you will save both yourself and your hearers.

2 Timothy 2:11-13 (New International Version) Here is a trustworthy saying: If we died with him, we will also live with him; if we endure, we will also reign with him. If we disown him, he will also disown us; if we are faithless, he will remain faithful for he cannot disown himself.

2 Timothy 2:14-16 (New International Version) Keep reminding them of these things. Warn them before God against quarreling about words; it is of no value, and only ruins those who listen. Do your best to present yourself to God as one approved, a workman who does not need to be ashamed and who correctly handles the word of truth. Avoid godless chatter, because those who indulge in it will become more and more ungodly.

Hebrews 6:10 (New International Version) God is not unjust; he will not forget your work and the love you have shown him as you have helped his people and continue to help them.

1 John 1:5-8 (New International Version) This is the message we have heard from him and declare to you: God is light; in him there is no darkness at all. If we claim to have to have fellowship with him yet walk in the darkness, we lie and do not live by the truth. But if we walk in the light, as he is in the light, we have fellowship with one another, and the blood of Jesus, his Son, purifies us from all sin. If we claim to be without sin, we deceive ourselves and the truth is not in us. If we confess our sins, he is faithful and just and will forgive us our sins and purify us from all unrighteousness. If we claim we have not sinned, we make him out to be a liar and his word has no place in our lives.

1 John 3:6 (New International Version) No one who lives in him keeps on sinning. No one who continues to sin has either seen him or known him.

1 John 3:16-18 (New International Version) This is how we know what love is: Jesus Christ laid down his life for us. And we ought to lay down our lives for our brothers. If anyone has material possessions and sees his brother in need but has no pity on him, how can the love of God be in him? Dear Children, let us not love with words or tongue but with actions and in truth.

"Now all has been heard; here is the conclusion of the matter. Fear God and keep his commandments, for this is the whole duty of man. For God will bring every deed into judgment, including every hidden thing, whether it is good or evil."

Ecclesiastes 12:13-14
New International Version

Printed in the United States
By Bookmasters